The
2 Bucket Rule

The Fastest Way to Peace of Mind

Carol L Rickard, LCSW

WellYOUniversity®
Publications

The 2 Bucket Rule
by Carol L Rickard, LCSW

© 2024 Carol L Rickard   All Rights Reserved

ISBN: 978-1-947745-47-6 (paperback)
ISBN: (Ebook)

WellYOUniversity®
Publications

A Division of Well YOUniversity, LLC
5 Zion Rd.
Hopewell, NJ 08525
888 LIFE TOOLS (543-3866)
www.CarolRickard.com
Carol@CarolRickard.com

Could "Hidden Stress" Be Stealing Your Happiness?

Take the

"What's Your Hidden Stress Risk?" Quiz

Tinyurl.com/HiddenQuiz

Contents

A Moment in Time

As I walk down the hallway,

I hear voices in the living room.

Not wanting to *interrupt,*

I *wait* for there to be a pause.

But as I stand there waiting,

I overhear what they're saying…

My father is dying.

That was 1976 when I was just **14.**

I never told anyone what I'd heard.

Instead, I cried myself to sleep every night,

and started drinking every day.

1

I always say:

If *anyone* knew how much I was

drinking back then, I most certainly

would have been put in rehab!

Drinking became **my way** of dealing

with the overwhelming stress.

Luckily for me,

basketball season came,

and I replaced drinking with basketball!

Since then…

My life's journey has taken me

to the people and places **I needed**

to learn healthier ways

of coping with life and overwhelm.

Today…

I am so grateful for the chance to share

with you the secret I discovered **along the**

way to creating *lasting peace & happiness.*

Why I Wrote This Book

It was a normal day at the office,

just like any other typical Monday.

That was *UNTIL…*

they stepped in to my office.

"Carol, I'm going to be leaving."

my clinical director said.

Then…

"And I've decided to retire."

my operations director said.

Suddenly, the team I'd worked with

for the past 3 years was *gone…*

And yet…

Somehow, I found myself

still feeling peace, *calm* &

a *genuine happiness for them.*

On my drive home, I started reflecting on

the day & how I did that.

I realized I've **trained my brain**

to navigate life's challenges

using these *2 buckets.*

That's when I decided I *needed to write*

this book to show YOU exactly

how to do that too!

About This Book

I doubt you have read a like this!

I like to use a lot of pictures, analogies, & word art which help information *stick* in the brain!

I call my approach:

SMARTheory™

(It's what makes my books and trainings *different* from all others!)

KNOWLEDGE is the *left brain* at work.

This is where YOU **know** what to do!

Since I use "pictures" & "images", I end up

tapping into the other side of the brain –

the right side!

With both sides working

on the same page,

the result is getting people to

Move knowledge into ACTION!

This book is designed to be more like

"a workshop in a book"

So, you walk away with tools to use!

How It Works

The Buckets

If you stop and think about it…

EVERYTHING in life

fits into one of two buckets -

 or

Sadly,

Far too many people waste a

great deal of their life energy

putting things into the

Could **you** be one of them?

The **key** is simple:

Make sure you're using

the RIGHT bucket!

This will help you DO just that.

1st - We look at *what* goes in each bucket.

2nd - We look at *how* to begin applying the rule in your own life!

Are you ready? Let's go…

The CAN Bucket

The *only* things that go in this bucket

are *the things* you *can…*

change

control

do anything about

If it **doesn't** fit these criteria...

Then it **must** go in the CAN'T Bucket!

The CAN'T Bucket

Anything & everything that does *not* fit

into the CAN Bucket must go here!

This means:

You CAN'T CHANGE IT!

You CAN'T CONTROL IT!

You CAN'T DO ANYTHING
ABOUT IT!

IMPORTANT:

Just because we put things in the
doesn't mean we're done!

A critical lesson I've learned along my way:

we must still **manage** the Stress Impact

those things have on us.
(more on this later!)

For example:

I still needed to immediately take steps

to manage the **stress impact**

of my colleagues leaving.
(which I did using what's in this book!)

Now let's move on *applying the rule!*

How To Use It!

Applying The Rule

There's good news & bad news!

The **BAD** news:

Our brains run on **"auto-pilot"**.

Basically, it means we go about our days

not thinking

and operating on a *'subconscious'* level.

People DON'T realize this until it's <u>too</u> <u>late</u>

and the **"auto-pilot"** is *causing issues*

in their health, career, & relationship.

This is usually when they come

to see me for counseling!

Now for the….

Our brains have this incredible power called

"neuroplasticity"

This means we can always RESET

our **autopilots** to better serve us!

BEWARE:

Just _doing something_

a couple times won't work…

It requires _doing something_ in **repetition.**

(Think back to learning to ride a bike,
tie your shoe, or even drive a car!)

Brainology 101

Research has shown how the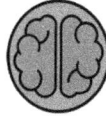

uses these things called "neurons"

to carry out all the work it does.

We have **86 *BILLION*** neurons in our brains

that talk to each other!

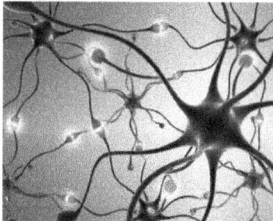

This "brain talk" happens when a neuron

sends an *electrical signal* to another:

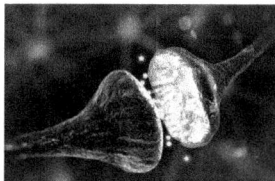

The reason this is important is because

Neurons that *fire together* –

WIRE TOGETHER!

↓

*The **more** they fire together,
the **stronger** the connections get!*

This is…

How we RESET our **auto-pilot**

& <u>build</u> new habits!

So, the more you apply the *2 Bucket Rule*,

your  begins to learn & set it as

a new **auto-pilot** - just like mine has!

Follow The Map

Hopefully by now you can our

brain has incredible power that can either

Help Us Or Hurt Us

Using the 2 Bucket Rule in your life

you're making sure yours is *helping you!*

Introducing the **Bucket Map...**

Following this map

will put you in *control!*

Connect

This is the **most important** step -

without it, <u>none</u> *of the others can be taken!*

Our **auto-pilot** can take us on DETOURS to

The	The
Past	Future

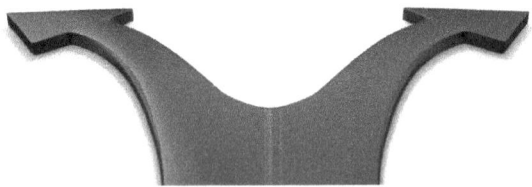

The problem is…

when we are **LOST** in one of those places,

We're **not** in the *one place*

we can WORK with our buckets…

the **PRESENT!**

We must stay

CONNECTED to the present *moment*

to apply the next step of **the rule,**

 What follows on the next few pages

are several tools I use to

STAY CONNECTED.

I want to encourage you to use

several of these tools *daily.*

Connect Tool #1

NOW Anchor

1) Find a stone that will fit easily in your pocket.

2) Write the word "NOW" on it with a marker that won't come off.

3) When you find yourself getting "lost", hold the stone & say these words:

$$N_{otice}$$

$$O_{nly}$$

$$W_{hat-is}$$

Taken from the *WordTools Series*

So…

DON'T have access to stones?

No problem!

Here's a **modification** you can use:

1) Take a stack of 4 quarters (or nickels) & tape them together.

2) Tape a little piece of paper around it & write the word **"NOW"** on it.

3) When you find yourself getting "lost", hold the coins & say the phrase!

And…

Here's 1 more **modification** to use:

1) Take an index card or a little piece of scrap paper.

2) Write the word **"NOW"** on it in really big letters.

3) When you find yourself getting "lost", hold the paper & say the phrase!

* I came up with this card idea for my

patients who'd have a custody hearing…

"anchoring" them

back to our support!

Connect Tool #2

Start paying attention to your:

Thoughts

Feelings

Behaviors

These will be the indicators you're

heading towards **"The Detours"**.

When you notice you're getting lost,

say the following phrase to yourself:

'Feel your feet!'

Both tools help ANCHOR you

in the present moment & pull you back

to TODAY!

Connect Tool #3

This tool I want to share happens to be

the **most powerful** of all!

I must confess…

I first learned it on the job **30** years ago -

But it wasn't until I received it as a

that I was able to **"live" it:**

One Day At A Time

This tool has magical powers!

But,

it's <u>only</u> *words* UNTIL it's put into **ACTION**

And this is how you do it…

First, read the following:

YESTERDAY, TODAY, and TOMORROW

There are two days in every week that we need not worry about, two days that must be kept free from fear and apprehension.

One is **YESTERDAY**, with it's mistakes & cares, it's faults & blunders, it's aches & pains. Yesterday has passed, forever beyond our control. All the money in the world cannot bring back yesterday. We cannot undo a single   act we performed. Nor can we erase a single word we've said – Yesterday is gone!

The other day we must not worry about is **TOMORROW**, with it's impossible adversaries, it's burden, it's hopeful promise and poor performance. Tomorrow is beyond our control!

Tomorrow's sun will rise either in splendor or behind a mask of clouds – but it will rise.

And until it does, we have no stake in tomorrow, for it is yet unborn.

This leaves only one day – **TODAY**. Any person can fight the battles of just one day. It is only when we add the burdens of yesterday & tomorrow that we break down.

It is not the experience of today that drives people mad—it is the remorse of bitterness for something which happened yesterday, and the dread of what tomorrow may bring.

LET US LIVE ONE DAY AT A TIME!!!!

(Author Unknown)

Second, take a blank sheet of paper &
write Yesterday, Tomorrow, & Today
on it so, it looks like this:

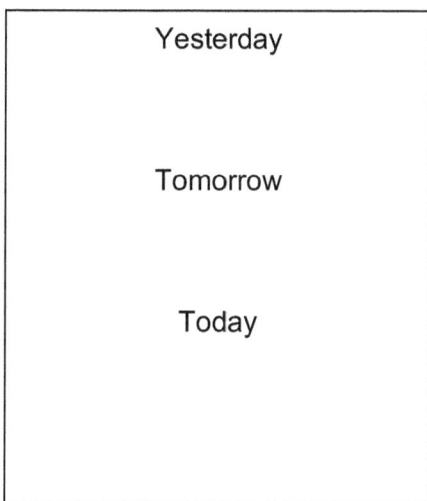

```
Yesterday


Tomorrow


Today
```

Under "Yesterday" –

- Write all the things on your mind
  having to do with the PAST.

This includes *regrets, resentments, hurts,
the I Shoulda-Coulda-Woulda's, Why me's*
& anything else stressing you out.

Under "Tomorrow" -

- Write all the things on your mind having to do with the FUTURE.

This includes *worries, fears, "what-if's", uncertainties, I Hope's, wants,* & anything else stressing you out.

Under "TODAY" -

- Look at each item you've written so far & ask yourself this question:

"Can I **DO** *anything* about that **TODAY?**"

If YES - write the **SPECIFIC** *ACTION*

you can *take* under TODAY.

If NO – Just leave it.

There is one last step to take!

- Fold paper back *& forth *just above* **TODAY**, gently rip apart on the fold.

 DO NOT
USE SCISSORS!!!

It is IMPORTANT to do it by your own hand.

You now have 2 pieces of paper.

Get rid of Yesterday & Tomorrow…

there is *nothing you can do with them!*

Hold on to TODAY

This is the only day

we *CAN* DO anything about!

Do this every morning & carry TODAY with you thru the day until you're able to live in TODAY!

Connect Tool #4

One last **POWER TOOL:**

"Mind Pushup's"!

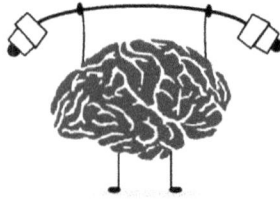

I used to think I *couldn't meditate*

because my mind wouldn't be **QUIET!**

That was until…

I met a Buddhist Tibetan Nun who taught

me what I'm about to teach you!

My teacher:
Ani Trime

She explained there are

4,000 types of meditation!

"I'm going to teach you the simplest one:"

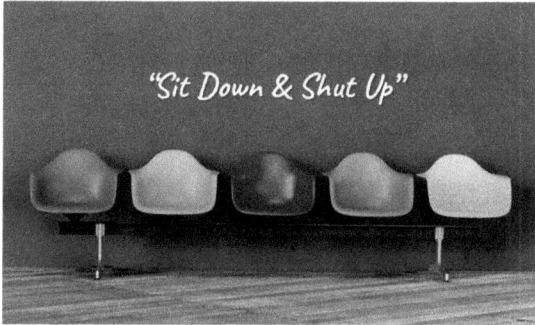
"Sit Down & Shut Up"

I remember thinking to myself -

'I can do that!'

The goal of **Mind Push-Up's** is to:

STRENGTHEN OUR

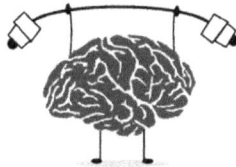

our **attention** muscle!

Do this with me **right now** –

(but only if it is *safe* for you to do so!)

- Sit comfortably.

- Set a timer for 1 minute.

- Close your 👀 or look down towards floor.

- As you breath **IN** –
  think…*"My mind is calm"*

- As you breath **OUT** –
  think…*"My body's relaxed"*

Use the video to help you practice…

Tinyurl.com/MindPushups

Assign

With EACH situation we face,

we MUST decide *which* bucket to put it in:

 or

And,

There's a simple ❓ to ask

to determine the RIGHT BUCKET:

Can I do anything about it RIGHT NOW?

There are only **2** answers:

YES or NO

If the answer is YES -

> Then *DO* what you CAN!

If the answer is NO –

> Then ***MOVE ON*** to the next step.

Remember:

Just because we put things in the CAN'T

doesn't mean we're done!

We must still **manage** the

Stress Impact

those things have on us.

I'd like to share *a few tools*

to help you <u>build</u>

your **"Assign"** muscles!

Once you're *comfortable* assigning buckets,

you can then move on to asking:

"Is this a CAN or CAN'T?"

NOTE:

If you're serious about wanting to have

peace and calm in your life…

Then you've got to **do the practice!**

There is NO "magic pill" or "magic wand".

The Full Plate Tool

This is a great first practice step to helping

you identify what's in your life right now.

Step 1   Write down **all the situations** in
         your life *causing you stress*.

Step 2   Now go thru each one & ask: *Can
         I do anything about it RIGHT now?*

Step 3   For each one you **CAN'T -**
         put a big **X** through it!

You can use the ACTION sheet seen below or
simply do this on a blank piece of paper!

How Full Is Your Plate?

Step 1: Take some time to write down all ALL the things you can think of in your life
that are causing your stress

** Be sure to include the BIG things as well as the everyday little things!

Step 2: Review each thing & place an X thru everything in the CAN'T Bucket!

Get your ACTION Sheets at:
FreedomFromStress.com/2Buckets

Serenity Stress Tool

I created this tool for my patients &

discovered I **needed** it more!

It's what really helped me get
my brain trained using the buckets:

#1   Make a list of ALL the things that
are stressing you out.

#2   Using the ACTION sheet, as seen on
next page, write the things on your list
in the section they belong.

#3   Fold the paper on the line and **RIP
IT IN HALF**. Throw away what you
CAN'T do anything about!

Get your ACTION Sheets at:
FreedomFromStress.com/2Buckets

43

The Serenity Prayer Stress Tool!

Grant me the **serenity** to accept the things
I cannot change:

_____

_____

_____

_____

- - - - - - - - - - - - - - - - - - -

The **courage** to change the things I can:

_____

_____

_____

_____

And the **wisdom** to know the difference

44

Take ACTION

Now that you've assigned it to the

we still need to do something!

1 mistake people make is

trying to ignore what they

CAN'T control or change.

This **won't** *work!*

A bucket *can only*

hold <u>so much</u> before

it *OVERFLOWS*

45

We must take ACTION to manage

the **STRESS IMPACT** it has on us…

I learned this lesson the *hard way* in 2002

when my CAN'T OVERFLOWED

& almost cost me my **dream** job.

Out of desperation to not get fired…

I accidently discovered the

LIFE CHANGING method

I'm about to share with you!

I call this life-changing discovery:

✓ RapidRelief Method
Anytime and Anywhere

I learned that when we use…

the right tools in the right order,

we can control stress & anxiety

anytime, anywhere in just seconds!

My promise to you:

If you will **USE** my method,

you too can CONTROL

stress & anxiety

anytime, anywhere in just seconds

to have lasting peace of mind!

Understanding Stress

STRESS is…

Our
Brain's
Survival
Mechanism

It is going **24** *hours a day*

& you CAN'T STOP THE PROCESS!

It's hardwired to respond to

changes or situations

to keep us alive!

It's kind of like your car alarm…

It's ALWAYS running!

PROTECTED
BY
ALARM SYSTEM

48

However, recent research has proven we

CAN *TAKE CONTROL* of this process.

It all starts with...

using the RIGHT

In the RIGHT order!

Now...

Think about how many

changes or situations

you face in just one day?

A LOT!

FYI! *STRESS* comes wrapped

in *a lot of different packages...*

Stress can be…

+

Winning $400 million Powerball! *(I wish!)*

or

-

Getting terminated from my job.

It can also be a…

BIG
change

or

SMALL
change

Leaving 2 minutes late!

Lastly,

Changes & situations can be either…

They exist!

or

Just a thought in our mind!

When it comes to stress - our brain has

3 basic responses...

But there's one more I've uncovered

during my **30+** year career...

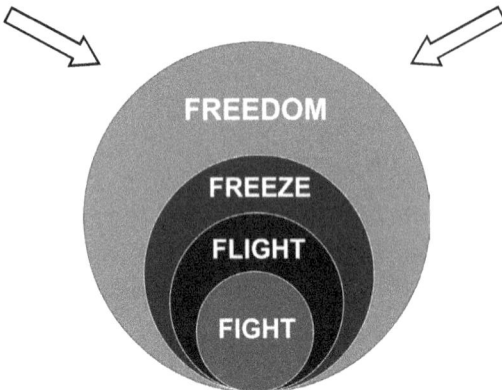

Taking action

stress no longer <u>negatively</u> <u>impacts</u> us!

More Brainology

Our brain has a built in "*alarm system*",

I call it: **The Defense Center.**

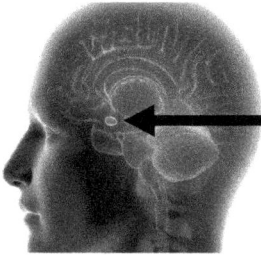

Amygdala
Sits deep in our brain.

It's *constantly* operating &

scanning our **environment**

for what it perceives as <u>potential threats</u>:

SAFETY = **Familiarity**

Our brains…

like things to stay the same!

When it detects a **change** or a

situation it's not familiar with…

It sounds the alarm!

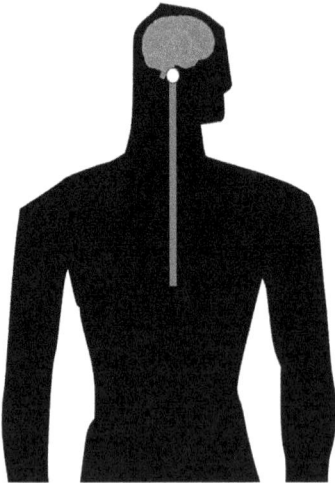

Defense Center
sends signals
& *energy to*

↓

Our Body
We can't stop this –
Only MANAGE IT!

And our "stress response" is turned on to:

Fight

Flight

Freeze

Here's an example…

Has this ever **happened** to you?

It's the night before
you leave for…

And You
CAN'T sleep!

That's because your brain

is *responding to the* **CHANGE**

happening the next morning!

Using the ⊙ Rapid Relief Method
Anytime and Anywhere

You'll be able to get some sleep!

A better way to think of

this process is to

think about a tub!

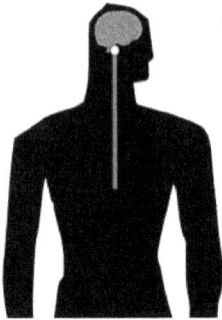

The Brain = Faucet

The Body = Tub

And a tub can only hold so much before it:

OVERFLOWS!

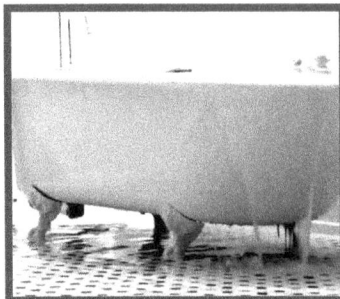

The Right Tools

What is the **only** thing that will

take-out Superman?

KRYPTONITE!

When it comes to stress, we all have…

Stress Kryptonite!

Science is very clear…

the fastest way to **STOP** our

stress response is *breathe…*

HOW *you do it* MATTERS.

There are a few ways

I want you to practice with me.

Do this test with me…

Put **1** hand on your chest &

one hand on your belly like this:

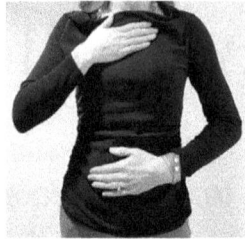

Take a breath & **NOTICE**
which hands moves.

(You might need to repeat this a couple times to be sure!)

I'm afraid I have some bad news if…

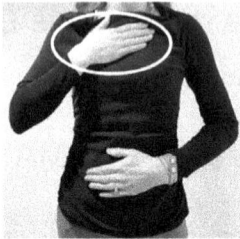

this hand *MOVED.*

This *won't work!*

We ***need*** to get air into

the <u>bottom part</u> of our lungs…

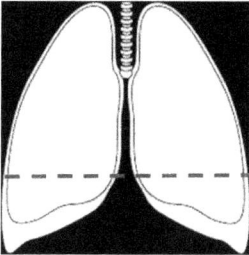

"Loading Dock"

This is where oxygen gets

"loaded" into our bloodstream!

It's like this…..

Versus…

So,

      Let's try this again BUT this time,

      concentrate on making

      the hand on your belly move!

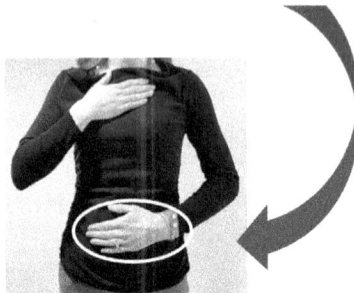

Ready? 1,2,3…*BREATHE*

Don't worry

If you don't get it *right away,*

it's something that needs **PRACTICE!**

A good way to do this:

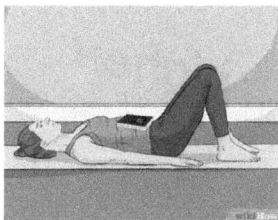

As you breathe in,
        try to *raise the book!*

Have you ever watched a sleep?

What *MOVES* when they breathe?

Right!!!! Their belly!

Here's the thing…

We're all born **"belly breathers"** –

Somewhere along the way *we **changed.***

I have a theory...

When our clothes started

*to fit a **little tighter**.....*

we started *sucking the air* up **higher!**

Have you ever heard that

Belly Breathing

&

Yoga Breathing

are ***good for our health***?

This is WHY!

S l o w i n g our *breathing*

will also **STOP** our stress response!

When **stress pressure** starts building up -

our **breathing** *starts*

SPEEDING UP!

It's part of the brain's **"HARD WIRING"**

designed to keep us alive!

Taking control of our breath

as you inhale & exhale

helps **OVERRIDE**

the stress response.

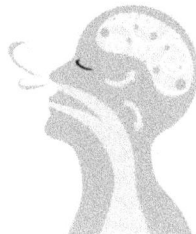

The RESET Breath

This is another breathing tool

backed by scientific research.

Do this with me **right now** –

Breathe IN:
(thru the nose)   S   L   O   W

count of 5

Breathe OUT:
(thru the mouth)   *S L O W E R*

count of 7

Do 3 Breaths!

Here's how it works...

When we SLOW DOWN our breathing,

Our 🫁 *signal our heart* to slow down.

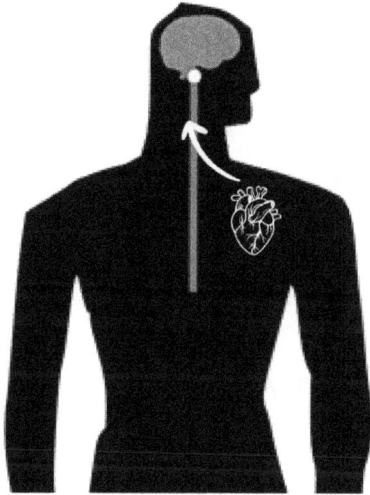

Our heart then *signals our brain* to

turn off the stress faucet!

Dump n Destroy

This is my **secret weapon** for managing

all my emotions from the CAN'T bucket.

Here's what you need:

- ✓ A piece of paper
- ✓ Something to write with

1) Simply **Start** *writing*

2) *DO NOT* READ IT

3) *Destroy IT!*

It's **very** different from "Journaling"

which can be another great tool!

*PS. You **CANNOT** use a computer or phone!*

The goal is to just *get it out…*

When you **read it**, you **RELOAD** it!

It *doesn't* make situations go away.

It DOES **decrease** 😊

the power of the emotion.

If **you're afraid** someone will *read it* -

Try this…

The Disappearing Dump!

- **Go in the bathroom**

- **"Dump" on toilet paper**

- **Flush it when done!**

Variations:

#1 - Dealing with Loss

This is my *dearest* friend I lost…

Hope Taylor

Nov. 2020

Honor Book

- ➢ Get a journal

- ➢ Put a loved one's photo on the front

- ➢ Write a letter to them as often as you like as if you were talking with them.

It's an *IMPORTANT* way

to **honor & release** the feelings.

#2 - Not Sure What You're Feeling

This is a great way to *Dump N Destroy*

when you're just **not** **sure**

WHAT you're feeling or thinking

(or you'll try to *read* what you write!)

Here's what to do:
- ✓ Get a piece of paper
- ✓ Grab markers, crayons, pastels
- ✓ Pick colors that match your feeling

Here's a few examples of one of my clients:

#3 - Can't Shut Off The Mind

It also works *well* when…

1) You can't **fall asleep** because your *mind racing*

2) You **wake up** at night & your mind is racing!

**IMPORTANT:

You must go write in

another room for it to work.

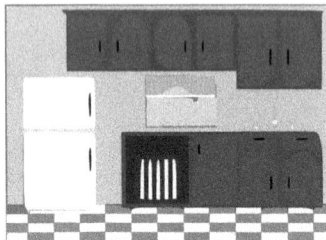

The kitchen is a good place to do this!

Don't turn on any

overhead lights.

(You don't want to wake your brain up!)

Instead,

Use the **stove** light or a **night** light.

Here's what to do:
- ✓ Go to kitchen
- ✓ ***Dump*** on notepad
- ✓ DO NOT READ it
- ✓ Go back & lay down

Don't be surprised if you *must repeat!*

(You may have ***A LOT to dump!***)

When you wake up –

If it's "crap" from the day before – ***destroy***

If it's stuff for the day to come – *USE IT!*

#4 - Anytime, Anywhere!

There's 1 more variation!

NO PAPER NEEDED…

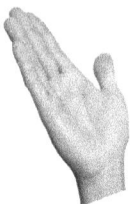

Your hand = **PAPER**

Your finger = **PEN**

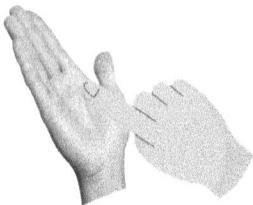

DUMP!

When done – blow it away!

The Right Order

Now that you have some

of the **RIGHT TOOLS,**

It's time to understand

the **RIGHT ORDER.**

Let me ask you a ...

How do you keep the tub

from overflowing?

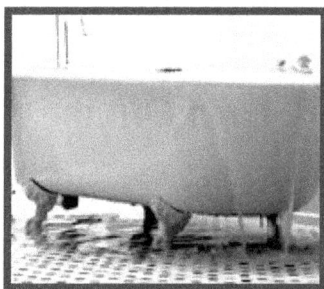

Most people I ask will say:

"Turn off the faucet."

But...

What happens if someone comes along

later and *"turns it back on"?*

If it is close to the top –

It will **OVERFLOW!!!!**

So,

There are really **2** steps required

to keep the tub from overflowing:

1st - *Turn Off* the faucet.

2nd - *Drain* the tub!

This brings us to the:

RapidRelief Method
Anytime and Anywhere

And the **2** simple steps we MUST **follow:**

Step 1 =

the level from
BUILDING UP!

Step 2 =

RELEASE
so the level drops!

Each step must be done *in order...*

Step 1 ➡ Step 2

These tools below can used to

(You must find the ones that work best for YOU!)

Read	Mind Pushups
Count to 10	Mantra / Quote
Step Away	Prayer
Listen to Music	Shower or bath
Breathing	Aromatherapy
Guided Imagery	+ Self Talk

NOTICE:

STOP tools are passive, **no energy,**

and...

engage your brain!

A Critical Point:

You MUST have tools that can be used...

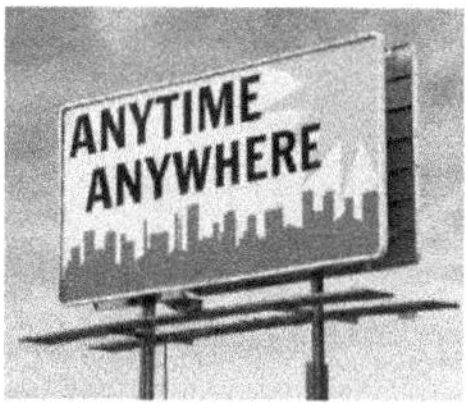
ANYTIME
ANYWHERE

and no one knows!

There are **3** powerful 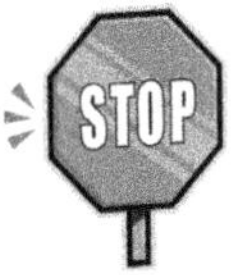
STOP
tools we

ALWAYS have *with us...*

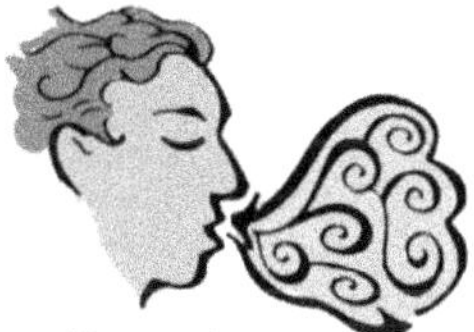

Breath

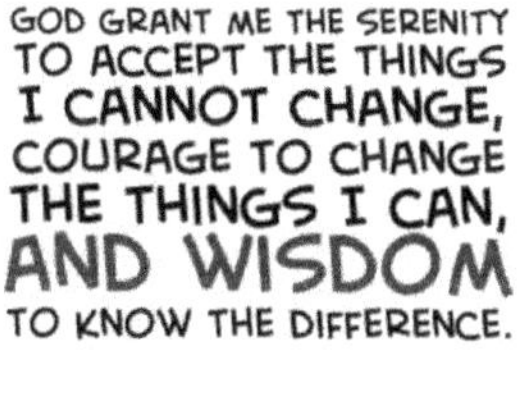
GOD GRANT ME THE SERENITY
TO ACCEPT THE THINGS
I CANNOT CHANGE,
COURAGE TO CHANGE
THE THINGS I CAN,
AND WISDOM
TO KNOW THE DIFFERENCE.

Mantra / Quote

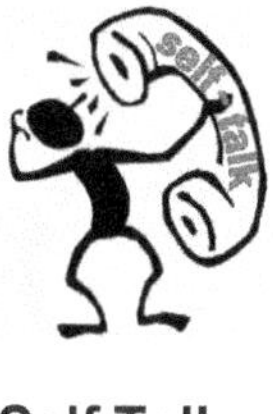
self talk

+ Self Talk

The tools below can be used to

(You must find the ones that work best for YOU!)

Talk	Coloring
Walk	Punching Bag
Write / Dump	Hobbies
Sing / Dance	Laughter
Clean	Gardening
Exercise	Ho, Ho, Ha, Ha

NOTICE:

RELEASE tools are active, **use energy,**

and…

engage your body!

A Critical Point:

You MUST have tools that can be used…

 and no one knows!

Here are **3** powerful  tools we

ALWAYS have *with us…*

Walk

Dump & Destroy

Talk

The method works because…

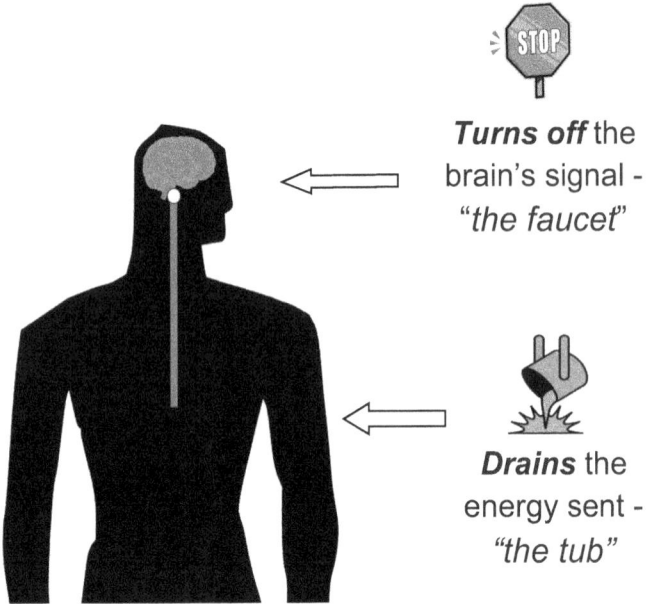

Turns off the
brain's signal -
"the faucet"

Drains the
energy sent -
"the tub"

Although discovered 22 years ago…

recent *advances* in neuroscience

now validate why it works!

Wrap Up

First…

We looked at the 2 Bucket Rule:

EVERYTHING in life

Will fit in to one of two buckets!

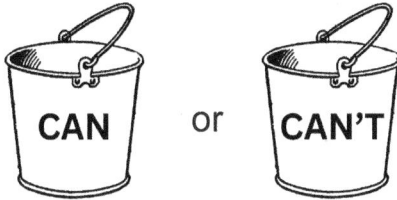

CAN   or   CAN'T

Then…

We looked at **WHAT goes in each bucket**

to make sure you're using

the RIGHT Bucket!

You DON'T want to keep

wasting any more of your life trying to

<u>control</u> things in the CAN'T bucket!

Lastly…

We looked at *HOW to apply the rule* &
introduced you to the **Bucket Map:**

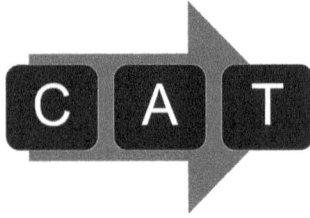

Connect

You must be in
the present moment!

Assign

Put in one of the 2 buckets:
Can or Can't

Take Action

DO what you CAN
or
MANAGE what you CAN'T

RapidRelief Method
Anytime and Anywhere

FYI!

Just as I am *finishing up this*

I had a situation happen that

required me to USE the **2 Bucket Rule!**

 My rescue dog – Bongo

escaped when the wind

blew the front door open!

By the time I realized what had happened,

I couldn't see him anywhere….

Thankfully…

I was able to stay calm,

keep calling his name,

& he came running several minutes later!

Will You Help Me?

Thank you for purchasing & reading my

I am **extremely** grateful and

hope you found value in reading it.

Please consider sharing it with friends or family

and leaving a review online. Your feedback &

support are *always appreciated*, and allow me

to continue doing what I love.

Simply scan the code below or go to:

Tinyurl.com/2buckets-review

Thank you!

Don't Miss This SPECIAL Offer!

Join Carol for the

Stress Smarter Masterclass

This 45-minute video training with Carol is a quick way to reinforce what you've learned!

ONLY $7

For A Limited Time…
SAVE $140

Tinyurl.com/bycarol

Need More Tools?!

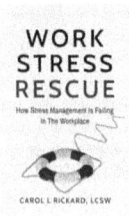

Work can be a challenging place! This gives you so many more tools to ensure your success in the workplace.

And Carol has written more "tool" books!

If you need help:

✓ Losing weight

✓ Dealing with anger

✓ Managing health issues

✓ Beginning meditation

✓ Practicing self-care

Take a look at the next few pages…

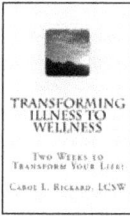

Chronic illness doesn't exclude you from having wellness. Get a blueprint to follow for taking back control of your health!

Are you sick & tired of feeling sick & tired? This is a step by step system for reclaiming your life from depression.

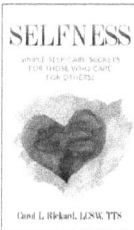

Self-care is often forgotten in this busy world. Carol offers simple and practical strategies to fit in to your busy life!

No – this is not promoting smoking! Instead, it provides the knowledge & the 'tools' to finally "Kick Cigarettes Butts"!

Available: amazon.com/author/carolrickard

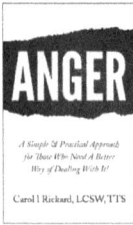

ANGER - one of the most
powerful emotions there is.
Learn how to manage it instead
of it managing you!

Losing weight doesn't have
to be complicated! Learn the *7
Laws of Lasting Weight Loss* a
car can teach us.
Guaranteed to work!

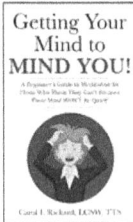

Your mind *is not* supposed to
be quiet! Learn how mediation
really works & change your
life forever!

Do you find yourself struggling
with what to say or how to help
someone you care about?
Learn how to say it & what to

Available: amazon.com/author/carolrickard

WordTools

What are words tools?
They are acronyms with purpose & meaning!

They are officially called *Artinyms™*, which is Sanskrit for "describe".

On the back of each wordtool is a question for you to answer should you choose to!

We have **4 different versions:**

Wellness Vol. 1 & 2,   **Self-Esteem** Vol. 1 & 2
Business Vol. 1 & 2,   **Athletes** Vol. 1

Examples:

The

Only

Day

Afforded

You!

A

Deliberate

Adjustment

Providing

Transformation

Daringly

Recognize

Experiences

As

Mine

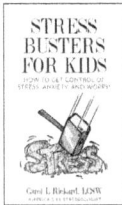

NEW RELEASE!!!!
Kid these days have to deal with so much stress. This makes sure they have the tools to succeed!!

We have three different versions of adult stress books because life circumstances can be different for each.

Choose the one that *best fits* your situation!

Caregiver

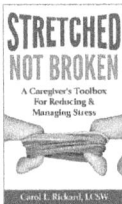

Research has shown caregivers are the MOST vulnerable. Learn quick, simple, practical tools for reducing and managing it.

Stress Eater

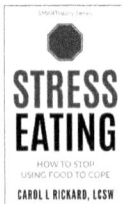

Do you find yourself eating when under stress? Get the tools & knowledge needed to break away from any old habits.

General

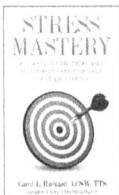

STRESS… It's all around us and NOT getting any less! Get the system Carol has taught to 1,000's & finally take control!

This series of books introduces Carol's proprietary method™ that you learned about in this book! Each version has added chapters geared towards that **specific audience.**

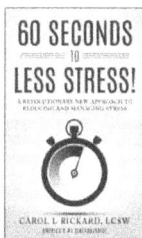

General Audience - This is the book that started the series! You'll learn the system that lets you finally take control of stress!

Brides

Nurses

Caregivers

Teachers

Available: amazon.com/author/carolrickard

About The Author

Carol Rickard, LCSW is a distinguished health and wellness expert dedicated to equipping individuals with the tools necessary to recognize and effectively manage stress. With over 30 years of clinical practice, Carol has developed a groundbreaking method that enables people to alleviate stress and anxiety in just seconds.

Her innovative approach extends to her recently developed quiz, designed to help individuals uncover "Hidden Stress" that may be impacting their mental health. This free 30-second quiz, titled "What's Your Hidden Stress Risk?" offers a quick and insightful assessment, guiding users to better understand their unique stress profiles.

As a stage III cancer survivor, Carol intimately understands the urgency of having effective coping mechanisms when life takes unexpected turns. She has authored over 25 books on stress management, sharing her expert knowledge and practical strategies to help thousands lead healthier, more resilient lives.

Her award-winning books, coupled with a nationally syndicated television show, have transformed the lives of many by providing real-world solutions to everyday challenges.

Speaking:

Carol is available to do both live and virtual speaking events. Contact her to get more details.

To Contact Carol:

Please feel free to reach out if you have questions or comments. She'd love to hear how this book has helped you!

Email:

Carol@CarolRickard.com

Connect with Carol on:

Linkedin.com/in/CarolLRickard

Facebook.com/CarolLRickard

Youtube.com/@CarolLRickard

www.ingramcontent.com/pod-product-compliance
Lightning Source LLC
Chambersburg PA
CBHW060952040426
42445CB00011B/1114
9781947745476